SPELL JARS AND POUCHES

Spell Jars and Pouches

ANUNG VILAY

Courageous Creativity

Contents

Introduction ix

1	Creating Spells	1
2	What Is Intention?	8
3	The Basics to Cleansing and Charging	13
4	Ethics and Appropriation	28
5	Protection	33
6	Love	41
7	Prosperity, Abundance, Success	50
8	Creativity	60
9	Growth, Change, Manifestation	66
10	Clarity and Confidence	72
11	Intuition and Magical Abilities	78
12	Happiness, Peace, Luck	85
13	Grief and Feeling Lost	91

14	Health	97
15	Not Truely An End	103
16	Resources	106

About The Author   109

Copyright © 2024 by Anung Vilay

All rights reserved. No part of this book may be reproduced in any manner whatsoever without written permission except in the case of brief quotations embodied in critical articles and reviews.

NO AI TRAINING: Without in any way limiting the author's [and publisher's] exclusive rights under copyright, any use of this publication to "train" generative artificial intelligence (AI) technologies to generate text is expressly prohibited. The author reserves all rights to license uses of this work for generative AI training and development of machine learning language models.

First Printing, 2024

Introduction

What a world we live in now. Where all the teachings of old and new are at our finger tips online and in books we can buy or borrow. I love it. I'm grateful that you picked up this book. While spell jars and satchels are just one small way to do spell work it has many options open to you.

You will not get bored.

Not going to lie, I'm a little lazy. This book is years in the making of me experimenting what can work or not with as little effort. Because I was in the trenches in the dark ages when there wasn't much out there for books for us fledgling witches. And yes, I was born before the the internet was widespread. (It's "official" birthday is in 1983, but did not get into public use until 1993.)

So what I could find out there was long, ritual-like spells. Especially coven ones. Which did not go well with this introvert. I am a solitary which through and through. Plus, it wasn't like I was going to find a bunch of other pagans in the 90s in the suburbs of Minnesota.

Surprisingly I did find some good books during high school in the county library system. And once I got my license I was off to the few occult shops in the big bad city. (According to some of my friends' parents.) Then everything opened up for me. All the books and supplies I needed, but also a community.

Though it did take me a while to really ask questions other then the basics. But knowing I had spaces and people to go to made me feel less alone. Even as a solitary witch you like to compare notes. Especially when you're young, you don't want to do anything "wrong". Even if you never get indoctrinated into other religions their trauma is everywhere. Seeping into our everyday lives and what others teach us in mundane life.

As time went on I figured out I was an eclectic witch. No specific teachings out there really called to me. Which seemed to track being mixed race, growing up with a bunch of other cultures, foods, languages, religions and in dozens of different school. Why not this too.

I read up on Greek and Egyptian mythology first (I mean who didn't have this stage). Hinduism, Druidism, Daoism, buddism, Taoisn, Shinto, Wicca, and so many others. I pretty much made it into my major in college. My senior paper was about trickster gods. Of course I've studied all the different ways of witchcraft.

But what kept calling to me were charms and talismans. Things you could make to have around your home or you could wear that have a specific effect.

Introduction ~ xi

Even in the fantasy books I read where someone would have a necklace that gave them the gift of elegant speech. Or someone who could charm their home to keep all harm away. We all wish for those kinds of absolutes, but we can work for that kind of magic in our own lives also.

Its just doesn't have the kind of flair we want.

In this little corner, your magic can go double as decoration in your home. Whether or not you have people who come over who you are not as open with about some of what you do in your life. It doesn't even need to be out for others to see for it to work. Its just for you.

If you have it in pouches it can be carried in your bag or in your pocket. Other ladies carry it in their bra. Some stuff in in their boots. Whatever floats your boat.

When you get farther along into your practice you can figure out what works with you and have your own personal pieces. These can be individual stones that you carry, jewelry, giant stones you keep in your home.

My flavor is jewelry and I get to support small artists at the same time. Mostly because that is not in my wheelhouse of creativity. Metalwork may be earth element but it is also fire and that is not my second element. Others like to make their own. Grow it or scavenge their own pieces.

This book is easy enough for beginners but can move you up to intermediate with what you put in, how much you combine into the jars, and other things we will go over later on. There will be easy steps but don't feel like you have to get complicated right away. Explore and see what works for you. Some things will be a little different for you with your own practice, symbolism , and upbringing.

Either way, have fun. Nothing I put in here will kill you. I think.

Chapter 1

Creating Spells

Spells can be a creative and complicated as you want or as simple. If you've watch anything about magic and witches you've seen a range of spells out there. While some of what is shown in *The Craft* (1996) and *Practical Magic* it does have its base in fact, Hollywood always has to add its drama. Nothing wrong with that, per se, but we already get a bad rap as it is with a lot a false shit getting thrown around.

Not to say all that jazz isn't cool to see. I wish the spells I did do had something I

could actually see happening and gave some kind of sparkle. But that's the

dopamine hit we all want in this day and age.

The two main things you need to for a spell are:

1. Intention

2. Direction for the energy to go

That may seem simple, but only the advanced practitioner can only do spells with just that. Besides, its just fun to have all the bells and whistles too.

So that is why we have other ingredients and steps. This can include saying a spell or incantation (whether or not repeated). It can even be one big production with multiple people that all have their own parts. While those can be fun to take part in they are not useful for the everyday.

So we will stick with a jar or pouch, some crystals, herbs, and other odds and ends thrown in. The next few chapters will go deeper into intention, cleansing and charging, and ethics. All very important parts to any practice and spell work. After that will be chapters on specific kinds of spells and what you can put in them.

Adding to Your Practice

In other chapters I'll go over working with the moon and stuff from different cultures. But if you are in the beginning of your journey (or somewhere in the middle and still really exploring) you may not know what else you can add into you spells.

While this book will not really go into specifics into

any belief systems or directions, I would like to make sure you have ideas to go off of. While I started off an earth witch, eclectic got added on real quick. None of the practices I was seeing out there really fit me. Not only because they required a coven. Some were too focused on particulars gods or set of rules.

So I took pieces of things that worked for me and others I made up as I went. Of course I made sure I didn't just took something that had meaning or history and disregarded it. Respect for other's beliefs and practices does not end just because I did not want to follow them. It was a lot of experimenting to see what would work.

A lot of what I learned at first was what was native for me and European, because that was what was available. But in college I added in some ayurvedic practices. Had a random class that opened a door for me. That showed me many different indigenous practices. Ancient Chinese and Japanese. When I say I'm eclectic, I mean it.

So my first goddess I worked with was Gaia then somehow jumped to Kali. I can hear the laughter of anyone who knows anything about that goddess. Just know it wasn't a choice but for some reason I love the chaos.

Though I mostly do not work with any deity. Preferring to work with my own energy and that of the objects I am using. If it is for something bigger, it corresponds with them, or they want in on the action then I bring them in.

But some do not have any deities in their practices. Some have spirits, guardians, or ancestors. There are so many variations out there. Or you could follow on specific order and stick to that only. There will be a Resource page in the back for further readings that I will add in that I found were good reads for different beliefs to start off with. So if anything sounded interesting to you you had somewhere to start.

In a few chapters will go over the mixing and ethics of it all. So don't go jumping in yet.

Book of Shadows or Journaling

At this time, it would be good to have a journal or notebook to jot down what spells you are doing and the outcomes. Some people go all out and have them as a Book of Shadows. With all their spell work, crystals, herbology, and everything they learn and try magically in there.

For some people that is anxiety inducing. Its too much like homework and are scared of doing it "wrong". That you writing in it wrong and not its not perfect and pretty anymore. That's why you journal it. Its just a place to dump things.

Then when you figure things out then you can make it all pretty in a separate book. That's what I do. I have a notebook that I dump all my spell work, doodles, and random magical thoughts in. Then split them up when they make sense or work out into their prospective journals. I have a witchy one, a divination one, and astrology/human design one.

But its nice to have a place to see what you have tried, a date when you did it, and the outcomes. Then you can see what you can do to tweak them. It could just be because you didn't do enough 'extra' stuff (more on that in later chapters) or were not clear enough in your intention.

This helps you see where you could have missed a step. Like using the scientific method for your magic.

How To Use This Book

A brief note what this book is not. It is not a substitute for professional help, whether medical or psychological. Many of the things in here are things to do together with your doctor. I will repeat over and over do not ingest anything here. Be careful with combining things. Have good air ventilation. Don't burn yourself or the house down.

This is not an excuse to not do the work. Where you just think you can do a spell and sit back and think the universe will just bring what you want to you. You have to actually go out to meet the love of your life. You need to make the products to sell for your business. You need to go for a walk to lose weight. Nothing is going to be handed to you.

Yes, I believe the universe is always working to help us. But it needs to catch a moving target. Not the person hiding under the blankets.

There are a lot of books out there about magic and I am grateful you picked up this one. Its a little niche but I will try to make sure you have the basics down. Because we all have magic in us. These are simple spells that use ingredients easily found that have their own energies that will add their own magic to your spells.

This is just the beginning of what you can be. Feel free to add in or take out what feels right to your own practice.

If something gives you a strong reaction I ask you to sit with it first before you throw it out completely. Think it over, maybe journal about it. Why did you have a reaction? I'm not saying its wrong to have a reaction, but to examine it. What was the feeling and why?

Was it part of an upbringing? Do you come from an organized religion background? Or do have some kind of formal training?

In the end you can still get rid of the parts you don't like. I do it all the time. I just want you to make sure your practice is done consciously. Not because you are running from something. Or you have some shame that was beaten into you that doesn't serve you.

Enough with the heavy stuff.

The next few chapters will be the basics on getting started. After that will be the specific spells. You can jump around if you want to what you need or what interests you (of the specific spells). At the end is a resources page for further readings.

No matter where this book finds you in your journey in your magical practice I hope its jumping off point for you have some fun and get creative with your spells. Try and learn some new things.

Chapter 2

What Is Intention?

It is the first step to the spell. You need to have this be clear before you get started. For some that is why they start off with a full cleansing and circle. It completely clears their mind so that they can concentrate on what it is they actually want for this spell.

I have a jar that is not just for creativity, but also to help with my writing. It also has concentration, a clear mind, opening myself to my muse. When I want to get real fancy and complicated I add in abundance and money since I want my writing to my full time income at some point. But that takes a lot more work and energy for you newbies. Work your way up to that after some practice. But you can just have one just to bring prosperity and abundance to yourself.

There is also protection for yourself or for your home can last longer then a week or month. While a spell can be for protection for your upcoming trip. It will end and be thrown out after the trip is over. It can depend on who you ask on how long a spell can last. So don't feel like you are wrong if you don't exactly see it this way.

With a jar everything can stay where it is. You just recharge it every once in a while (more on that in the next chapter). To refresh you might take some things out or add more but there will be no need to get rid of anything.

Though at some point you will want to start over. Taking everything out and cleaning and cleansing the things you can reuse. Throw out the things that cannot be reused like herbs. Then start over with a base and add and recharge like before. I do this for all my permanent jars at least once a year. Mostly because I feel like some jars just get better the more you add to them and charge them in some instances. And sometimes my jar is just too full.

Setting an intention can be a simple or complicated as you want it to be. Though if you do have one for love, for example, once you do find someone and are secure you can make a different jar to have open communication or to strengthen the relationship. With prosperity many people will keep their jars even if they get a raise or a big influx of money. Who doesn't want more money?

Setting an intention is essentially adding energy to

something. You are giving it a job to do and giving it a boost to work towards that. It only lasts for a short amount of time so that's why they need to be recharged. Which is great so that after use you can reuse crystals for other things.

Manifesting

For most things this is the same as manifesting. Manifesting is not specifically connected to the metaphysical or spell work. It is putting thoughts and ideas out into the universe to enact change. The main definition is to make a thought a reality. So only just a little woo woo.

The concept has its foundations in several philosophical and religious traditions, from Hermeticism and Transcendentalism to Hinduism. Ultimately, it aims to put the individual in the driver's seat of their own life and makes them responsible for the positive and negative effects in their lives.

But it is only the beginning. With manifesting, as with intentions jars, this is the first step to get what you want. It does help you have a clear picture of what you want and you put energy into it. But that is not the end of it. You need to do the work. Send that out into the world then actually do something.

Doing manifesting helps you to focus as well as get the Universe's help. Then you need to take specific steps to work towards it. If you are looking for love then ask some of your friends to get a group together to either meet up with their other friends' single friends. Or go out together to mingle. It you are looking to get more money start going to networking events, polish up your resume, and apply to new jobs.

Hell, there's that Italian story of the man praying to God to let him win the lottery and God finally tells him you need to buy a lottery ticket first. You put the energy out there then keep building on it while its building in the Universe. Then when it comes back for you, becomes likes attracted to like, they give more.

So you need to know what it is you want to manifest in your life, set your intention (on that step), ground into that (next chapter), then working towards those goals.

Setting Your Intention

After you have cleansed you jar you start adding things in. For each section I will give a specific intention, but for here I can to give an over view of how to add it.

Some of the simple ways to set your intention is literally speak what you want and you add each piece in. These can be as simple or elaborate as you want. Some people like to have something that rhymes or have a poem. Just saying "six figure income" or "bring my soul mate to me" can be enough. It is the emotion and *energy* you put behind it.

This energy can be what you raise within yourself or what you pull from around you. While you are charging you also set the intention for the ingredients being placed into the spell. When ingredients get placed into the jar you set the intention.

While each ingredient can be a bit different in their strengths, which you should play to, adding your own energy to them activates them for their job to work towards what you want. You set the intention for each individual thing, then set it for the whole spell to seal it all together. Then when you recharge it later, add things in you also do this too. It is an exchange of energy.

Chapter 3

The Basics to Cleansing and Charging

There are many ways to charge you jar. Each individual component that gets added can be charged specifically as well as the whole jar (or satchel). Some can be chosen for the intention or what is easiest at the time. There are some that would not be advised for specific things. There are some crystals that you do not want to put into water or sunlight. Its could either damage them or the water could turn toxic to you.

You can decide how much or little you want to put into this. With every part with making your jars and satchel you can do as much as you want. It will not make it stronger or not, it needs to be in alignment to you energy and needs. Sometimes I go all out with charging my crystals in the sun and moon phases. Make moon water, have mantras and symbols carved into candles. And other times I put my crystals on the windowsill, not even knowing what the moon phase was, gave some energy and plopped it into the jar.

Yes, those ones that I put less energy into did not have has much to work with. Not that it didn't work. It is a balance between being kind of lazy some of the time and doing no work at all.

You still have to have respect for you practice. I'm just saying we do not need to go gung-ho know the exact moment the moon is full, create a circle of protection, and call on any and every god and goddess out there with offerings. You do you bo. We all got busy lives and only so much energy. Your spiritual practice does not have to be every day. It does not have to be a big production.

Some things can be done ahead of time. With creating your jars it doesn't have to be done all at the same time.

Sage

If you can find ethical sources for white sage I have found that most Indigenous Groups have no problems with people using sage for cleansing (I do not like using the term smudging since I am not of the practice). But using any kind of garden sage also works just as well. So does rosemary and dill (though some do not like the smell of burning dill).

Lighting the sage until the ends are red then goes out and smoke comes out. The smoke produced is what you use to cleanse with. Passing the object you want cleansed through it. Or if it is something bigger covering it in smoke. As with a room, making sure you get to every corner. Though with a person you do not need to completely cover and possibly suffocate them.

Incense

Incense have been used since ancient times for cleansing. Like saging, you are using the smoke from the incense to cleanse. Some types that are great: frankincense, myrrh, sandalwood, dragon's blood, and cedar.

Selenite

Selenite has been used to clear a person's space and aura. To cleanse other crystals and tarot decks between readings. Placing the item on the selenite overnight will be enough to cleanse.

Sound

The ringing of bells in many cultures have been used to keep evil away. In many Asian cultures they place them on the ankles of babies for protection. Using bells or singing bowls can cleans a space of negative energies. In a pinch people have banged on their pots to banished evil spirits from their homes.

Soil

Other things you can use to cleanse is to put them in the dirt or a potted plant. Some bury the item in the ground or pot. Usually overnight to cleanse it or for a full 24 hours. You do have to watch the weather on this if you do this outdoors if the item cannot come into contact with water.

The Moon

The Moon is mostly known for putting energy into things then just cleansing. But it is a source for this too. If you do not have any of the other options available you can use the moon to cleanse as well as charge your items for your spell. You will just be putting more into it yourself.

Salt/Water

Honestly, this is recommend a lot but I don't tell this to beginners. It can easily go wrong. There are a lot of crystals with different components that change or dissolve coming into contact with salt, water, or salt water. They can also damage certain crystals. You should also never cleanse any raw or natural crystal this way. Some specific crystals that cannot come into contact for long without being damaged:

- Amber
- Calcite
- Kyanite
- Malchite
- Moonstone
- Opal
- Selenite
- Topaz

Grounding and Protection

Grounding is so that before and after you do any magical work no excess energy is less in you. You do not want any stray energies added into your spells that do not belong and you do not want anything lingering to mess up the rest of your day.

It can leave you over energized for hours make it hard to sleep, or just have your senses off kilter. Its not only spellwork that can get us off balance. It can just be regular things in our personal lives, illness, and emotional turmoil.

Growing Your Own Roots

Imagine your energy extending down through your legs and sinking into the earth, becoming roots and burrowing into the soil to trade energy with the earth.

(This can be done standing of sitting.) Feel the earth's energy flow up into your body, filling you all the way to your head and then back down and out through your roots. This energy will cycle through you and clear away any excess energy as well as solve any energy deficiencies you might have. If you can do this bare foot and outside that would be great too.

Go For A Walk

Getting out in nature, especially if you can walk barefoot, will allow your body to trade energy with the earth and equalize your energy levels. Walking in nature also helps to build mindfulness and create a sense of ease in your life!

Connecting with the earth in any way can be a great way ti ground. Standing in the grass. Touching a tree. Playing in the dirt.

Water

Water is a conductor of energy. by sitting with your feet in a stream, your hands under a running faucet, or drawing yourself a bath can equalize your energy very quickly. Playing in the rain can also equalize your energy but if it's sunny out visualizing rain washing your energy clean will work just as well.

Wind

If you can go outside when it is windy this will work great. If not, sit comfortably and begin to visualize your energy body. When you have a solid image of it in your mind imagine a strong gust of wind blowing your energy around you, removing blockages, carrying away excesses, and refueling any energetic deficiencies.

Stones and Crystals

This should not come as a surprise that some crystals and stones have grounding qualities to them. Holding one and wearing some as jewelry can release energies and ground you. Examples are hematite, red jasper, black obsidian, black tourmaline, and smokey quartz.

Now, if you are a newbie you may not know all the information out there about why people use protection and shielding when doing spellwork. There are many different beliefs out there and again not the place to real delve into here. I just want to give you an overview and direction.

Many do believe that others' energies can cause us harm, whether on purpose or not. That there are non-human beings out there (spirits, angels, demons, ghosts, etc) that can mess with us and with our lives. So there are ways to protect and/or shield ourselves sometimes.

Stones and Crystals

Again, this is an easy one. There are crystals that have protective properties. Check out the chapter for examples or the books given in the Resources at the end.

Talismans and Amulets

Talismans include jewelry with a magical or religious symbol, runes, herbs, planetary squares, and medicine pouches. Some Hermetic traditions use very elaborate talismans with ancient languages and planetary sigils. Many amulets can be purchased at local businesses. A very personal talisman can be created by an individual for a unique purpose, and be made of feathers, clay, beads, fiber, and/or metal.

Just so you know, the pouches you will be making later in this books are technically talismans and amulets. So if that is how you want to ground protect yourself you can just to that section (after the next chapter, though it is the first spell chapter so you don't have to go far).

Candles

But using color magic (black) or writing protective words or sigils into a candle can make it a protective item. Then burning it can provide protection while burning it and after. You can also buy or make more complicated, extra mojo, more to it go for it. You can literally deconstruct a spell jar to be a part of a candle or around it to make it into a protection spell (or any kind of spell).

Light

In certain situations you can visualize light coming from within yourself or even arising from the east light a sunrise. Surrounding you with its gentle protection. Make sure it covers all of you. It does not need to be a bright light to blind everyone away.

Putting In Your Energy (Charging)

This is really the only step you need to do for each piece of your jar. All the other parts (minus cleansing) are just extra that you want to do or feel like is needed. There are several ways to put you energy into things. Though some of these steps are going to be a repeat of before with the cleansing there will be more to them. Cleansing you just do it, while the charging you have to put the intention in for what you want the spell to do.

In a lot of magic you are told to place things in your dominant hand to pour the energy or intention into it. For most that is your writing hand, but not always. A trick I've learned which one that is is to quickly clasped your hands together. Which thumb is on top? That is your dominant hand.

Or you can just cheat and use both hands.

Up to you. Since we are not doing anything high level with directing this energy anywhere.

One way to feel your own energy/magic to be placed into an object is to imagine heat or light coming from your heart. You concentrate your focus there until you feel you have enough. Then draw it down to your hands, either to pool there or go straight into the object. The object can be in your hands, you can be touching it, or just hover your hands over.

As you add in the energy/magic you can have a word, saying, or mantra you are either saying or thinking. If you can feel what that means. If you want protection think about a locked door, being warm and safe in your home, or the feeling of a hug. If you want love have those feelings you associate come to mind. What things are you doing with this love?

Remember, you are setting your intention here. This is the part here that each part that gets put into the jar (or satchel) has what you want it to do. As well has the whole jar. You want it to bring in money, luck, and abundance. Or protect your home and keep harm away.

Aphantasia is the inability to voluntarily create a mental picture in your head. So it means that some people cannot actually visualize in their mind. Other ways to add energy would be to use your other senses. The feeling of holding the hand of a loved one. The feel of luxurious clothes. The taste of a chef made meal. The clean smell of a new car. The warmth you feel in wrapped in a blanket, protected.

Other ways is using word association or emotions might work better then picturing things. The emotion behind the word is the important thing.

The Sun

For certain crystals just bathing in sunlight can give some great energy. Some of the energy is for growth and reflection. To some it has more "masculine" energy, which is associated to strength, work, success. This does not mean that the Moon, being feminine energy, does not have these but more as a balance to each other.

Some stones do not do well in the sun. The worse that I've heard of is that it can fade out the color.

The Moon

The full moon is widely thought as the best time to charge your crystals. But you don't have to wait weeks just to get close to that. Each phase has its own properties and energies you can use. Holding your crystal (or other objects) in the moonlight with draw in the the energy. Speaking or thinking what you want for your crystal as you put it in the path of the moon will guide the energy to what you want.

- New Moon
- Waxing Crescent
- First Quarter
- Waxing Gibbous
- Full Moon
- Waning Gibbous
- Third Quarter
- Waning Crescent

The new moon is know for beginnings. This point up till the waxing gibbous is drawing something to you. This is where you set your intentions and build towards them. You check in with yourself and on the progress you have made to keep the momentum going.

Waxing moon is the beginning after the new moon. A time of ebb and flow. It can relate to fertility or life and death. It can also be associated with spiritual growth and transformation.

The full moon is the grandmother of times. This is best for charging anything really. It is the time to re-adjust but also to celebrate. It is also a release. It is the climax if you started something during the new moon.

During the waning time is more for slowing down. With it being the phase after the full moon. This is when you reevaluate what you were working on. This is when you release what was not working and make space for the next cycle. The perfect time to rest and regenerate. Find inner peace and reconnect with yourself.

Of course all these meanings can be nothing for you. The moon will still give energy no matter what stage. I have had times where I just threw a few stones I knew I needed for a spell the next day on a windowsill just to charge it. Gave it its intention and left it for the night. Nothing else special to it. I couldn't even tell what phase it was.

When I can I will have these extra things because its important to me. But if you do not follow in those beliefs or you don't care to have any of that flare then don't. Some days I want all the candles, crystals, and herbs. Done during the "right" sign and moon phase; outdoors, barefoot, and with a bonfire going. Other times its just a single candle and one stone. They all work. All you need is the intention.

Moon Water: You can also make moon water at this time. Put water in a bowl or glass on a windowsill or outside under the moon. It will charge under that particular moon phase and if you charge it. But you do need to bring it inside before the sun can touch it. Use this to add extra energy to your spells.

Other Phases: Other phases you can use are the days of the week or the seasons. Those are easy to search for online or there will be books in the Resources at the end.

Oil, Incense, Candles, and Symbols

There are specific kinds of these that you can buy. A money oil or love candle. Many are made with the herbs, oils, or crystals that are already shown within this book. Incense made out of Dragon's blood for protection. Again, these are not necessary but add more oomph. Oils that have the herbs given in other chapters will give the same qualities.

This the same things with the incenses and candles. On top of this you can use color magic. There are general colors that you would expect associated, like green for money and prosperity, pink for love. More associations will be given for each section.

Symbols are another thing and I do not have the space or time to get into it here. They can be a simple as the dollar sign or a full on sigil. I will give some references in the back to where to learn further about these. You can carve these into you candle. Draw it with the oil or in the air. You can draw it on a piece of paper and your jar can sit on top of. If you're feeling fancy you can even buy grids and symbols on cloth or carved into stone and wood to use.

For some they do invoke a deity or spirit also into their practice. That, again, is a whole different book for you to check out. But if that is not something that calls to you you do not have to have it in your practice. Even if you do have one they don't even have to be called upon all the time. But do know that this is an option to have.

Sound

Saying phrases or mantras, music, and other sounds is another great option. As said before, this is a great option if you cannot visualize. Its also for those who are uncomfortable with saying things out loud or you would get weird looks from the other people you live with. There are so many playlists online on Spotify and Youtube for whatever theme you want.

Many of these can be subliminal as well so you can just have instrumentals or beach waves playing but the message underneath has what you want. Or you can just have regular music that have any words or feeling you want. Once, to recharge a prosperity jar I played Rihanna's *Bitch Better Have My Money*. It's however you want to put the energy in.

Chapter 4

Ethics and Appropriation

More metaphysical ideas and views are being accepted and shared then ever before. Which is great for people to be more open to new ways of knowing. But the main problem that pops up is taking something from a native group and making it your own without respecting it. Or taking so much that most people cannot partake anymore. Or completely changing it from its original form, not give any history to it, and act like you created it all on your own just for money.

The difference between appreciation and appropriation is the respect behind it. Are you acting like you came up with it? Are you learning the history behind it? Are you using it the way it is intended? Are you actually listening to the professionals (especially medical) about what ways it can be used? Does it come from an open or close practice?

If you do not know what an open or closed practice is stop what you are doing and learn about that first. Not just about the item you are thinking you are using but about the culture and everything associated around it. And don't give me that bullshit that you had no idea or that no one told you. Nothing is in a vacuum. We all have the internet and social media. We can ask people what something is. If it is closed then you do not get to use it unless you get permission. Honestly, for me, I just don't use it because I can easily find an alternative.

Now there are some areas that can be seen as grey. Some are closed because of their communities like the Roma, the Amish, and Haitian Voodou. Others try to be closed because their belief have been poached so much its eroding their knowledge. We have seen this too much with sacred Indigenous practices use of white sage smudging and the use of palo santo. To the point of some communities losing access to their sacred plants.

Companies have taken over the land where it grows, over-harvesting it. To the point of damaging the plants on the surrounding land and other vegetation. On top of that exploiting the local workers paying them slave wages. All so they can overcharge people to cleanse themselves in a belief system not their own.

There is more then one way to cleanse. I have personally been invited and taught by a Native Shaman about smudging. I live in Minnesota so can easily get sage locally. But I do not always do it. What I am doing does not always call for it. Which is a purification process for a space, object or person of energies, thoughts and emotions.

For many Indigenous groups its not just sage, but cedar, sweetgrass, and tobacco. You might also not want to burn something just because of other health reasons (allergies, asthma, living in an apartment, etc). Other things you can use for cleansing are your garden variety sage, rosemary, selenite, bells, or singing bowls.

You have an obligation to do right in your own practice. Especially when you are working with any set of gods. There are plenty of stories out there of people not respecting a belief system, god/goddess, or entity and having karma biting them in the ass. Just don't do it.

Take just a few hours to look things up. You are reading this book so its not going to kill you to read I little more.

Getting your supplies

Not to say there are not ethical ways to use them out there. But you have to do some research and too many do not want to do any work. And if you only want to have fun and spread light then this book is not for you. Stick to your little woo woo stuff. Nothing wrong with surface level stuff of crystals and sparkly things, but you don't get to just take anything just because someone wants to sell it. We as consumers need to take a stand somewhere with our money at some point

Sometimes you don't need to get the newest thing or what's popular right now. Especially when it comes to crystals you should definitely be reusing them. Herbs can be burned and mixed with salt to make black salt; allowing for one more use. Getting rid of it can be just thrown outside, back to the earth.

The farther you get into learning, hopefully, you will find people to start talking with about where to get supplies or how you do spells. Though the internet has been a great source to allow others to learn so much more, there has been a lot of misinformation thrown around. As well as a lot of fake things out there.

It is really easy to get duped with fake crystals. Even with seeing picture and videos, great reviews, you just never know. I know veterans who go to gem shows around the world who sometimes have to really examine a specimen to tell its a fake gemstone. What you see is also not always what you get sent either.

Make sure you look around for your supplies, not just for what is cheap. Sometimes you need to get things that can be reused over and over then the ones that you will throw away. There are plenty of places you can find quality for great prices.

On top of that, finding something that fits your aesthetics and can be placed out as decoration is great too. Why not have something that can work as more then one thing.

Chapter 5

Protection

Protection is one of the most basic thing us humans have always wanted in life. It is something we can never really guarantee. We want protection for our home, while we travel, for our family, and even spiritually.

Not that I believe that people are hexing left, right, and center all the time, but people put back energy out into the world without even knowing it. They talk badly about each other, sometimes to the point where its all the time. That kind of energy can latch onto you, that obsession.

Though there will be ways to protect yourself from hexes and the evil eye here as well. There are also other entities out there that can be harmful here and on other planes. Sometimes its just from physical harms from stupid people in the world. Bad drivers, accidents, people being forgetful are just a few things we all have to look out for on the daily.

Another thing about being protected in being grounded. Just like in a storm, when lightning strikes, the building is protected by a copper cord grounded into the ground. Or if you have a strong foundation a strong wind will not blow you down.

I always make a jar for when I move into a new place. I have one for in my car. I carry one in my bag that moves all the time because they change around depending on what I'm doing in the day. I make them as gifts for friends. Because I care for them but its also something pretty for them to have.

Home protection jar

Now I have done a lot of moving in my life so I have made so many of these. Like, a lot. And each one has been different. Depending on what I had, how much money I had to get supplies, where I could put it, and what the space called for. Each home has its own spirit so take your time getting to know where you live before you make this jar.

Some of my own personal things I always place in my jars for crystals are black tourmaline, clear quartz, and selenite. For herbs, it's rosemary and sage since I always grow them or have them on hand. And for the other items

are nails. I try to have nails that I already own and some that are from around the home also that I cleanse.

That is just the base and I add depending on what the home needs. Plus as time goes on it will get added to to be recharged or redone completely. So you don't need to worry so much about it being perfect.

Don't forget to take each item in both hands and set you intention before placing it into the jar. You can have some fun with some of the things you say. I always have a least one thing that's somewhat serious just to make the right point gets across.

Shield this home from energies that do not serve those within it
All acts of negativity repelled
No bad vibes allowed
All who dwell here are safe from physical and spiritual harm
Bitches be gone

Travel protection satchel

Having a simple satchel that you can carry with to protect you while traveling is always helpful. We are always going places. On buses to school, driving to work, trains, or planes for vacation. You can have this in your pocket, bag, or luggage. Believe me, it won't be the weirdest thing security with see if they search you.

I always put in red jasper, black jade, and clear quartz. If I really feel like I need it then I will put in black tourmaline and amethyst too since you'll be around a lot of other people and their influence. So you will need to stay grounded and clear headed. Sometimes I will put in a stone from my home in there if its for a specific trip. So I know I will come home safely.

I try to not use herbs if I'm traveling on a plane. Security gets a little upset when you bring plants and herbs on a plane, especially abroad.

Crystals

Amethysts are well-known crystals for protection and stress relief. It is known to bring its wearer clarity of thought, relief from grief, protection, and wisdom. It can also help protect you against other people's projections and keeping negative energies at bay.

Aquamarine protects its bearer from harm.

Citrine is a powerful protection crystal that reduce stress and exhaustion, leaving its wearer with a feeling of calm that radiates throughout the body. They are also notable crystals for protection against mercurial mistakes leaving their wearer with a clarity of thought. Placed under your pillow, Citrine can ward off bad dreams and aid with a night of more peaceful and restful sleep.

Black jade can help you tap into your intuition and steer clear of negative people and situations. Sometimes it can be difficult to see where negativity is coming from, but black jade can help you tune in to the root source.

Black obsidian carries a calming and positive energy that can help you remember to look on the bright side of things.

Black tourmaline is a powerful protector stone with the ability to ground a space and clear it of negativity.

Clear quartz is helpful in both deflecting negativity and attracting positivity.

Jet is used in protection, grounding, and purification. It has the ability to aid energetic cleansing and is even used to heal damage to the aura. it is also used for warding off evil and its protective ability includes warning off nightmares and dispelling fear.

Moonstone is one of the best protection stones, named for the celestial ruler of the night sky. Moonstone is an amazing crystal that soothes and calms its wearer by dispelling cosmic fog and negative energy. Known for its karmic healing, it has been used as a protective talisman for travelers for generations. This stone is known to aid in focus, awareness, and even to enhance psychic powers.

Obsidian is used for grounding protection and eliminating energy blockage. It also helps with guarding against self-sabotage. It can also protect you against negative self-talk and judgment.

Opal is one of the best stones for protection against negative energy as it is a highly reflective stone. Opals are powerful protection crystals that will pick up on thoughts and emotions, magnify them, and send them back to you. Opals can also absorb the energies and vibrations of people around you, including negative or harmful ones, and reflect them back to their source.

Pyrite helps shield you from the harmful effects that technology can have on the mind and body.

Red Jasper is used for protection for travel. Whether that is in a car or plane, long or short distances.

Rose Quartz is one of the most dynamic crystals for protection known to be helpful in both deflecting negativity and attracting positivity.

Snowflake obsidian wards away negativity and any psychic attacks. It is also good for grounding, releasing negative emotions, and easing anxiety.

Herbs:

Angelica is strongly associated with protective properties. Carrying its roots can protect against evil.

Basil is placed in bundles in the home for protection, usually in the corners. In your jars you can use fresh, dried, or incense (though I would not recommend fresh since they would mold if not dried properly).

Bay Leaves (Laurel) is a powerful protective,

cleansing, and banishing herb. It has been used to ward off negativity and ill will. There is even a practice to that has it protecting against lightning strikes. Burning it can clear away active curses or even keeps hexes from reaching you.

Black pepper can be used to protect the boundaries of your property and to repel any negative energy.

Cedar has traditionally been placed above the front door to keep out negativity and ill will.

Dill, dried or fresh, has been used for protection and to bind magick. It was also used to protect the home and from nightmares.

Elder is highly revered and to some is seen as holy. To the point of only harvesting after getting respectful permission. All parts can be used for protection from its leaves, berries, flowers, and sticks. There are even stories from history that those living even near an elder tree are within its protection, even pets and livestock.

Garlic was worn by the ancient Greeks to guard against illness, theft, and possession by evil spirits. It can also be used for cleansing and banishing

Rosemary has long been used to protect the home to ward off negative energies. It was even referenced in the movie Practical Magic to be planted by your front door. It is a good alternative to White Sage for smudging and cleansing.

Sage is used for cleansing, protection, and granting of wishes.

Other:

Nails from you home, especially one you just moved into can be used buried outside the home. In folklore iron nail, mostly because common people had access to these, use these to protect against fairies or the fae folk.

Horse shoes has long been used in folk lore for luck and protection. Many place above their door to ward off evil, misfortune, and bad luck.

Egg shells are protective since they are a barrier from the inside of the egg from the outside world. So it creates a that negative energies cannot pass through.

Salt has been used to create barriers against evil since the ancient times. Choosing which kind you use will add extra properties to your spell.

Chapter 6

Love

We all need a little love in our lives. Some from others and some from ourselves. Of course, the main disclaimer with love spells is that we will not be forcing someone to fall in love against their free will. We will be drawing love to ourselves. Building love that we already have.

Sometimes things might go wrong because the people around us are not what is good for us. But that's the thing about magic, it gives you what you need not what you want. So if you are trying to strengthen your bond of your family it might have to break the one for your significant other because they are toxic for you and you won't see it. Which in turn will let you build up your friendships more. The heartbreak sucks but you are better off in the long run.

Love can mean many things. So many of us want romantic love. Its shoved down our throats (no pun intended) that it should be the goal in life to have a life partner to pop out crotch goblins with and live happily ever after with. But there is so much more to it out there. There is family love, whatever you make of family. Friendships and the many different levels of companionships you allow into your life.

I personally make a self love spell jar more since that boosts my confidence, which will have a better effect to bringing in a potential partner over a love spell. Also, who doesn't want another friend? (Well, some of the time. I am an introvert so I can't handle too many friends all the time.)

I want to reiterate here again that magic does not follow any denomination, but consent is still a must. We are not forcing someone to fall in love with us. We are asking the universe (or what ever gods/goddesses/beings/spaghetti monsters we believe in) to bring what we are asking for into our lives, in whatever form that is needed. The optimum word is "needed", not what we want.

We may want that shiny thing but we're gonna get what we're gonna get. The thing is, later on we see that it was the much better choice and things turn out so much better and we are much happier now then we ever thought would ever be.

Self love

A good place to keep this jar is either in the bathroom by your mirror or where you have you lotions

SPELL JARS AND POUCHES ~ 43

and things you use in the morning and evening to get ready. You will be looking and touching your face a lot during this. A time where you can add a little extra love to yourself.

Clear quartz and rose quartz is always a good base, plus lapis lazuli and malachite for balance and support. Lavendar and rose petals for their sweet scent and to show yourself some love. Adding in other parts is up to you.

While you get ready in the morning or evening you can also light a candle or pamper yourself extra to add a little extra magic. Keep an eye out for oils or lotions with the herbs given below. Not only do they give magical benefits, but cosmetically.

I am beautiful inside and out

I deserve all the love in the world

I am grateful for who I am and cannot wait for who I will become

Crystals

Amethyst does not just attract love but the right love. It also helps to solve difficulties in relationships and help to keep an open mind.

Azurite is suited to improve relationships. It produces a calming state and opens doors of communication, allowing the third eye to engage. Balancing emotions, it can transform situations and relationships in order to move them in the right direction.

Carnelian is a great crystal for supporting relationships (and a healthy sex life). It's great for promoting happiness, joy, and creativity—all great things to cultivate in your love life.

Clear quartz is a stone that can support a lot of intentions whether you want to amplify loving energy, repel negative energy, or simply clear your mind. This can also help us clear our connections, ties, and bonds whether to make them stronger or to help us see that we have outgrown them.

Chalcedony promotes kindness, goodwill, and harmony. Essentially a stone for friendship. It contributes to feelings of serenity and helps mediate emotions in groups, which can can discern the subtleties in group relationships leading to to balance and understanding. This is not only good for friendship groups but also school sand work settings.

Garnet is an excellent stone if you're feeling a bit ungrounded or insecure in your relationship. It can support you in keeping your boundaries firm while also helping to remove your inhibitions about exploring your soul's true desires.

Green Aventurine is ideal for the later phases of a relationship. It's linked to the Heart Chakra and can help you get through the ups and downs of a long-term relationship. It is great for rekindling long-term relationships or assisting individuals in opening their hearts to new partners after heartache.

Jade creates trust and support for healthy growth of a relationship. It also soothes your emotions if you're anxious about your partner's fidelity because it improves trustworthiness between couples. Wearing or carrying a piece of Jade in your pocket will allow its energy to enter your Heart Chakra, bringing you calm, balance, and good fortune.

Lapis Lazuli brings clarity and adequate support in the pursuit of love.

Malachite can help you feel stable, safe, and secure in opening your heart up to all types of love.

Moonstone is used for unrequited love and to reunite lovers who had parted with anger. It can make your love connection stronger and last forever.

Peridot can be used in promoting harmony within significant love relationships such as marriage and domestic Partnerships. Helping to open the heart and soothe emotional upsets.

Red Jasper can be used to strengthen relationships, particularly long-term ones. It can also help a person see past disillusionment in order to make their own choices.

Rhodonite can be pretty useful if you're dealing with heartache or attempting to negotiate the dating scene. One of the most effective stones for resolving emotional trauma. Rhodonite may also be used as a first-aid stone to help with emotional pain and anxiety. This stone assists the bearer in overcoming feelings of envy, anguish, and other harmful emotions following a heartbreak. It also offers the bearer the ability to forgive and reconcile traumatic problems gently and honestly. Some people believe that Rhodonite is a stone that will wake you up, especially if you're in denial about your existing relationship.

Rose quartz energy is a lovely heart-opener that aids in the cultivation of love, forgiveness, and compassion for others as well as for oneself.

Ruby attracts love, incredibly loyal and deep commitments. It enhances the ability to give and receive unconditional love.

Sunstone keeps our sensual essence from lying dormant within us and encourages it to flourish outward instead. It carries the revitalizing energy of the sun, it has the ability to bring light back into our life.

Herbs:

Basil has been used in love spells for centuries. It can be used to add commitment, build passion, or draw a new relationship to you. It can also be used to soothe lost tempers and ease discord between people, not just partners.

Calendula has properties for love. It can help you gain admiration and desirability.

Cardamom warms and gently stimulates the body and mind with its exquisite aroma and was often used in Eastern aphrodisiacs.

Catnip leaves have been used for luck in love affairs. It is called a Woman's Love Herb because it is said to make women enticing and charming.

Cinnamon is believed to increase passion and strength.

Clove was used by the ancient Romans, Greeks, and Persians in love potions or charms. You can use it you attract love and strengthen relationships.

Gardenia, according to the Victorian language of flowers, was give to someone to say: "You are lovely." They symbolize love, peace, healing, and spirituality.

Ginseng attracts love, luck, and health. The Chinese have used ginseng for thousands of years, believing that it enhances sexual performance increases energy, and eases stress.

Hibiscus symbolizes love, lust, and divination. In many countries, this is the flower of love, and it is used in perfumes and to make wedding garlands.

Jasmine is known as a symbol of love and romance. A traditional belief is that jasmine penetrates the soul and opens up emotions. It is still a favorite ingredient in perfumes all over the world.

Lavender folklore is about love much of the time. It was said to attract men but was also used for chastity. It has been used to attract a devoted partner and has been woven into bridal bouquets.

Lily of the Valley (also known as the May Lily) means "return to happiness" and most often symbolizes chastity, purity, happiness, luck and humility.

Misletoe hung over your door draws love to you.

Women having trouble conceiving would place leaves in a sachet. The Druids hung mistletoe to bring abundance their way.

Marjoram used in love spells will strengthen the love. To attract your future lover and fall in love by placing the dried herb or drops of oil in the four corners of your bedroom.

Orange Blossom symbolizes innocence, purity, fertility, and lasting love.

Roses are a classic for a reason and are linked to love. It was sacred to Venus, the Roman goddess of love. Still to this day it is gifted on Valentine's day and any day to loved ones. Using color magic go with red and pink to associate with love.

Ylang Ylang elevates the spirit and consoles the heart. It has an intense sweet, sensual, euphoric aroma.

Other:

Candles (pink or red) for their color magic representing love but also the flame.

Hearts for obvious reasons. Using the shape for symbolism.

Knots, especially love knots are recurring themes in jewelry, handfasting, and clothing. The Celtic love knot is an ancient symbol that represents eternal love through an interlacing design which seemingly has no beginning or end.

Shells being the holders of pearls or their symbols of Aphrodite/Venus.

Chapter 7

Prosperity, Abundance, Success

Prosperity, abundance, and money were the very first spell that I ever did. You would think as a girl it would have been something about love. But anyone in my life wouldn't have been surprised. I was only kind of interested in boys, but I was very interested in doing things with my friends and books. Which costs money. And the Capricorn in me never wanted to be broke.

Of course, having abundance is not all about money. It is about having our needs being met and not struggling. Having enough love, food, energy, and many other things for life. Not having to worry about things breaking in your home all the time. Having quality food nearby. That is the whole point of life, is to be able to enjoy life for ourselves and the people we care about.

Opportunity for all should be available no matter what but sadly is not the reality. We have to work with what we have. Part of being good is sharing what we have as well. I am not saying that we should be generous just because it means we will get more in life. Just that I believe in karma.

It's always good advice to not be a dick.

Having my dad's side of the family being Asian money is a big part of the culture. It's in the blessings we give to newborns, newlyweds, and graduates. That they get lots of money and share it with their family.

So it was very different for me to hear other beliefs and cultures that were so hushed about talking about wanting more money or even congratulating others on getting it. That we should all feel guilty about it. Cause that was never my upbringing.

Now we never really talked about the nitty gritty either. Don't get me wrong, they weren't progressive either. Just that money and the wanting of it was never a sin. It's a necessity of life. Having more of it makes life easier.

Money Jar

A good base for any money jar is citrine, green aventurine, pyrite, and tiger's eye.

Then add in some cinnamon, ginger, and some coins and any money you want. I always love adding in carnelian because most of my work is creative. Lapis Lazuli, moss agate, and jade are great choices too. Sometimes on a full moon I will write a wish on a bay leaf and burn it (sometimes with a green candle), putting the ashes in the jar. another good base is rice.

I am worthy of financial security and all the joys it brings.

I am a magnet for prosperity, and it flows toward me effortlessly.

Wealth constantly flows into my life.

Abundance is my divine birthright, and I claim it now.

Crystals:

Amber has associations with wealth and manifestation. Its golden hue makes it ideal for spells to invoke prosperity and abundance.

Amethyst is associated with the planet Neptune and is known for its ability to attract wealth and prosperity into your life. These crystals are also thought to help promote intuition and psychic abilities.

Bloodstone is used to overcome obstacles and clear paths in business and legal matters due to its ability to strengthen the mind. It is also thought to help increase your wealth and abundance. It is effective in removing fear that causes blocks to success.

Blue Topaz is associated with the planet Uranus and is known for its ability to attract wealth and prosperity into your life. They are also thought to be helpful in promoting creativity and change.

Blue Sapphire is great for manifesting wealth, luck, and prosperity. It can also help protect you from negative energy that can prevent you from reaching your dreams and accomplishing your goals.

Carnelian is the stone of good fortune. It is a crystal that is said to help promote motivation, creativity, and abundance. It is also thought to help improve relationships. They are also thought to help promote courage, strength, and other good things in one's life.

Citrine is one of the most prominent manifestation crystals because it transmutes negative energy into positive energy. It helps to promote optimism, increase energy levels, and attract abundance and wealth into your life. It is also known as the merchant's stone, the money stone, or the stone of abundance. It eliminates blockages which helps feel confident, meaning you will be more likely to manifest your dreams.

Cinnabar is associated with the planet Mercury and is known for its ability to attract money and wealth into your life. It is also thought to help with communication and self-expression. It can be used to improve your career and business goals. (Warning: washing hands after handling. Do not inhale or ingest.) As a business owner, place one (in an airtight bag) into your cash register to attract more sales to your business.

Clear quartz is one of the most versatile crystals. They are said to help promote a clear mind, energy levels, abundance, a positive attitude, and overall good energy. They are also thought to help relieve stress and anxiety.

Emerald in their lesser quality can be used for prosperity and abundance. Emerald crystals are associated with the planet Mercury and are known for their ability to attract wealth and abundance. This green stone is also thought to help promote intelligence, communication, and success.

Garnet is associated with the planet Mars and is known for their ability to attract money and wealth into your life.

Green Aventurine is also said to help stimulate creativity and manifest desires. The green coloring also represents the energy of abundance. It helps attract new opportunities, wealth, good fortune, success, expansion, and prosperity into your life. It is also thought to be a stone of protection and can help to keep you grounded during times of change.

Hematite is a crystal that is said to help promote focus, willpower, and abundance. It is also thought to help reduce stress and anxiety. It is a great crystal for people who are always on the go. Hematite is a great crystal to use for manifesting your desires.

Iolite is a wonderful crystal to use alongside other crystals for prosperity and abundance such as pyrite and aventurine. It helps promote clarity and organization and is useful in times when responsibilities are growing.

Jade is associated with the planet Saturn and is known for their ability to attract wealth, luck, and prosperity into your life. It is also thought to help promote wisdom, balance, and healing. The green jade crystal along with the green calcite are two of the best stones to help to improve your overall health and well-being.

Lapis Lazuli is a blue stone that is often used in meditation for its ability to connect you with your higher self and the spiritual realm. Promotes wealth, abundance, and prosperity. It is also thought to help you achieve your goals and live your truth.

Malachite is said to help promote prosperity, abundance, and success. It can be used to help enhance your career and business goals. It also increases life force and success and inspires confidence.

Moss Agate is a crystal that is said to help promote abundance, success, and prosperity. It is also a good crystal to help increase your fertility and improve relationships.

Peridot is a crystal that is associated with the planet Jupiter and is known for its ability to attract good luck and prosperity into your life. It is also thought to be helpful in relieving stress and anxiety. It can also help to increase your self-esteem and promote positive change.

Pyrite is a golden-colored mineral that is often known as fool's gold, the abundance crystal, or the prosperity stone. This is one of the money crystals that is said to promote wealth and abundance and is often used in money spells and rituals.

Rose quartz crystals are associated with the planet Venus and are known for their ability to attract love, happiness, and prosperity into your life. You can use rose quartz crystals to manifest your heart's desires.

Ruby crystals are associated with the planet Mars and are known for their ability to attract money and wealth into your life. Rubies are a beautiful crystal that helps to promote passion. They are great crystals to use for manifesting your desires, and bring you vitality, power, and the energy to get things done.

Sapphire is associated with the planet Jupiter and is known for its ability to attract money and wealth into your life. They are also thought to help promote wisdom, truth, and peace.

Sunstone is a crystal that is said to help promote abundance, success, and prosperity. It is also thought to help increase your energy levels and bring happiness into your life. Sunstone is a great crystal to use for manifesting your desires.

Tiger's Eye, also known as the lucky crystal, is a crystal that is said to promote abundance and prosperity. It is also thought to help you stay grounded during times of change and keep you focused on your goals. Tiger's eye is a great crystal to use for manifesting prosperity.

Turquoise is associated with the planet Mercury and is known for its ability to attract wealth and prosperity into your life. They are also thought to be helpful in promoting communication and self-expression. It can be used to help improve your professional goals. It is also used to channel leadership qualities. This can be a great stone for business owners.

Herbs:

Basil has been used in pockets and doorways of businesses to attract wealth and draw in money. It has also been given as a potted plant as a housewarming gift to bring love, prosperity, and safety to a home.

Bay Leaves has been used for manifestation and wish making, usually by burning. It is also used for wealth, abundance, and creativity.

Cedar have been placed in wallets, purses, or pockets to draw in wealth and prosperity.

Cinnamon is a well-known ingredient for prosperity and money. Many use it in the beginning of the month to blow good fortune into your front door or place it above your door. You can use this in powder, chip, or stick form.

Dill can be used to attract love and abundance,

placed in shoes for luck and success during important moments of your life. Placing a sprig in a change jar or in your wallet can bring success, wealth, and abundance.

Ginger brings a "hot and fast" element to money spells. It adds power to success for money and prosperity spells. Placed in purses, wallets, and pockets to increase wealth.

Lemongrass brings good luck and dispels feelings of hopelessness, despair, and lethargy.

Mint brings financial growth and prosperity. Some say that's why where money is made is called a mint.

Pin Trees are a sign of prosperity because they never fade.

Rosemary is a great addition for manifestation and success.

Rice has been considered a symbol of good luck, wealth, and prosperity for centuries. It is also symbolic of success, fertility, and good health.

Sage energy brings prosperity and protection over the home. Blue sage is often used for abundance rituals, money and prosperity spells as it is believed to attract wealth and success.

Other:

Coins or any kind of money is great to use to draw in more to you. It doesn't even need to be real.

Gold in many countries and cultures attract more wealth and prosperity because it contains the Sun's energy. The Sun is the center of our solar system, making all things drawn to it. So we want to draw all good things to ourselves the same way.

Green Candles attracts abundance and prosperity using color magic and the element of fire. You can also carve in symbols or words into the candle to add more power.

Chapter 8

Creativity

You don't have to be an artist to want to have more creativity in your life. It can be useful for any part of your schooling or work. Coming up with a new marketing idea or even just how to handle the new hire that just won't take the hint. Sometimes the normal things just won't do so you need to get a little creative and not get in trouble.

Creativity is also something that is overarching for artistry and making. Things that we create, either with our minds or by hand. This can also lean in the trades and sciences all the way to schooling. There are a lot of parts to helping your creativity that isn't just the artsy side. We all play games as kids. Many of us cook on a regular basis. Hell, many of us have had to get out of conversations we don't want to be in without wanting to seem rude.

Not going to lie, this is my favorite kind of spell

jars to make. Every time I find a new stone I look to see if it could be used for anything creative or artistic. I literally had to edit down my list for this chapter I know some obscure things that could be used here.

Since I have a creative business and am a writer I actually have two different jars and a pouch to take with me traveling. One jar and the satchel is a more of a basic one just for creativity so that I make sure all the energy I put into it is for that alone. The other one is more complicated since it mixes not only creativity but also artistry, focus, innovation, concentration and a little bit of business and money in there.

Yes, you can mix some things together into your jar but don't get too complicated. You can always make another. If you think it can all go together, like my business one, then go ahead. But if you want something for school, then for love, then you're worried about your car that's not all going to work together. Magic works better with a clear path. Give it a simple job so all the parts aren't fighting each other.

Writer's Jar

The base of any jar for me is green aventurine, rainbow flourite, citrine, and carnelian because they are so easy to find. I also personally love amazonite, apatite, garnet, celestite, lapis lazuli, moss agate, pyrite, and tiger's eye. For herbs I usually
put in rosemary and hibiscus because I grow them, sometimes using sage and bay leaves.

Other fun things to throw in there in a representation of your art. I was gifted a miniature journal that I use in my jar. Paint chips, crayon, paper with a poem written on it, or a page from your favorite book are other good examples. Whatever inspires you and represents what you want to do.

My creativity is wild, abundant, and free.

Creativity comes easily to me when I let go and let flow.

When I trust my intuition, my creative juices flow.

I am at my creative best when I shed the desire to please anyone but myself.

Crystals:

Amazonite improves communication and enhances creativity. It filters information that is processed through the brain and the intuition helping with all artistic pursuits.

Amethyst helps with expression, getting over doubt and a stronger connection to our wisdom.

Apatite inspires creativity and forward momentum. It can also increase inspiration.

Aventurine (green) is a crystal of inspiration. It activates creativity and can push in periods of creative growth. It is also used for good luck, fortune, productivity, and success.

Bloodstone heightens intuition and increases creativity. It also calms and revitalizes the mind, dispels confusion and enhances decision-making.

Blue topaz crystals are associated with the planet Uranus and are known for their ability to attract wealth and prosperity into your life. They are also thought to be helpful in promoting creativity and change.

Carnelian stimulates your creativity. For the artist in you it connects to the sacral chakra, which motivates creative passion, sexuality, and bravery.

Celestite enhances creativity and mental clarity. It opens one up to possibilities, new ideas, and dreams.

Citrine helps to instill concentration and focus, which are key in getting projects underway. A stone of joy and abundance, citrine helps you to interact creatively with the world. It promotes inner calm.

Fluorite enhances intuition and creativity. It also promotes mental clarity and focus.

Garnet stimulates passion, creativity, and determination. Helping us past our jealousy and self doubt to boost our confidence.

Herkimer Diamond excels in bringing in new energy and creativity. It will also help you recognize the blockages that are stalling your creativity as well as your spiritual growth.

Howlite can help with with self-awareness, creativity and improving ones emotional attitudes. Lifting your mood and promoting positive energies.

Lapis Lazuli enhances artistic talents and creative expression. Promotes honesty, authenticity and integrity.

Malachite is a stone that inspires confidence and creativity. It is also a stone for clarity manifestation abundance and success.

Mookaite Jasper balances inner and outer experiences. It encourages versatility and openness to new experiences, helping you to choose the right path.

Moss Agate enhances focus and can promote creativity. It is also great for emotional balance and grounding.

Pyrite helps with confidence vitality and creativity. Even though it is known for wealth and prosperity most people want their creative endeavors to bring in money

Tiger's Eye enhances creativity and bringing out ambitiousness in a person. Also great for accomplishing goals and lifting your mood.

Herbs:

Bay Leaves are said to promote inspiration and creativity. Sacred to the muses and useful for artists, poets and writers

Chamomile is great for clearing your mind, focus and productivity.

Hibiscus can unblock your art. Stimulating your artistic expression, passion, and productivity.

Lavender helps creativity by being open-minded

and clear headed. It can also help you explore your thoughts and emotions, and to be able to express them.

Peppermint stimulates creativity and helps to reduce fatigue.

Rosemary is a wonderful support to creative practices. It enhance memory and cognitive function, and also believed to promote a sense of calm and clarity.

Sage invites creative energy, clears your mind, and promotes inspiration.

Tea Leaves (green tea) promotes relaxation and focus, providing a serene atmosphere for creative exploration.

Other:

Copper has a high vibration and stimulates energy flow which embodies the quality of creativity.

Paper and Pen or any writing or art supplies. Adding pieces of the art or creation to represent what you want to make will had strength to the magic.

Chapter 9

Growth, Change, Manifestation

Even though all of these jars are about manifesting, there is sometimes a need to have an extra oomph. As with everything else, this is drawing something towards you. These are more things not so specific or concrete. You want a change but not quite sure what kind of change. You don't want to be where you are, just not here.

We all want to grow, to change to be better. Just overall. That is the point of growing up. Even as "adults" we should never feel like we are done. I interpret the Bob Dylan quote *'If you're not busy being born, you're busy dying'* as meaning if you do not continue to learn and grow you are not truly living.

So you want to make a big change in your life but you don't have any particular direction. This can be a good place to start. Yeah, you could go for money or happiness but you want something bigger. Something more for your life. Without blowing everything up. This a way to bring what is out there to you while staying grounded and not being knocked over by it all.

Take your time. See the synchronicities being shown to you. Journal about them and feel what calls to you. The best part is you can try things out for a while to see if they feel right first, then if they don't move on to the next thing.

That's the best thing. We are never stuck (other than children) with these choices. Don't get stuck in the sunk cost fallacy. It doesn't matter how much time or money you put into something. Move on when you are done with it.

Take the lesson from it and move on.

Manifesting Change Jar

I like using amethyst, black obsidian, Botswana agate, and howlite. My go-to herb is bay leaves. Also good to add are clear quartz, green aventurine, jasper, and malachite. I also take the time to sit out (when possible) to charge this.

Especially in nature around water and trees. Both represent the cycles and

life and nothing can stay the same. Even over time, it may seem like things look like nothing is different. But if you take the time you will see all the little details of what is new. Then over more time, you will see the major changes.

That is the same for us. Not everything is a huge transformation. Honestly, our bodies can't take it. Slow and gradual gives you time to adjust but also make sure things stick. Use the water to cleanse yourself. If you feel called, take a leaf to add to your jar.

I believe in myself and my abilities.
Thoughts shape reality, and I choose positivity.
My mind is open to new ideas and experiences.
I release thoughts that no longer serve me.

Crystals:

Amazonite brings good luck and is a stone of manifestation, especially when paired with the spoken word.

Amethyst is great for your journey of self-discovery or spiritual growth giving us clarity in our decision-making in manifestation. It's thought to provide clarity and insight, helping you to better understand your emotions and the deeper aspects of your experiences.

Black Obsidian teaches you to honor the imperfections of being human and to embrace your flaws and weaknesses as opportunities for growth and development.

Botswana Agate helps to raise awareness of the collective consciousness and the oneness of all of life. Encouraging deep contemplation of the circumstances of one's life that have led to strength, spiritual growth, and inner stability.

Clear Quartz can aid personal transformation and growth. Since it is incredible versatility and its ability to amplify positive energy it is also great for balancing and harmonizing.

Green Aventurine is the good luck stone that brings in new opportunities and beginnings. It is especially beneficial for those seeking to manifest fresh starts or embark on new adventures.

Howlite aligns all the chakras, balances them, cleanses them, and enhances spiritual growth. It also promotes tolerance and clarity of thought.

Jasper is valuable during times of transition. It imparts strength and grounding energy. It is a stone of acceptance, whether this is of new beginnings or opportunities.

Labradorite invites the potential for personal growth, transformation, and a deeper connection with your true self. It is ideal for those seeking to manifest more creativity and spontaneity in their lives.

Malachite is very grounding and releases negative emotions and emotional blockages. Associated with transformation and healing, it may assist in emotional healing, personal growth, and positive transformation.

Moss Agate is a powerful conduit of growth, development, birth, and creation.

Fire Agate ignites a personal transformation through self-reflection. It is a stone that calms the body and provides a sense of comfort and security.

Shungite is very grounding and stabilizing which can be good during times of change. It encourages you to learn more and push forward.

Herbs:

Bay Leaves (Laurel) are great for manifesting. If you've been on social media for a while I'm sure you've seen the videos about writing wishes on a bay leaf and burning it on a full moon. Well, it's actually true. The moon part isn't necessary, but it does add some power to the spell.

Cherry Blossom Tree symbolizes growth, renewal, and the fleeting nature of life. The short time they bloom in spring symbolizes new beginnings and rebirth.

Cinnamon will increase the power and success of your spell.

Dandelion is resilient and adaptable, representing growth and transformation.

Holy Basil helps us in times of change. Medicinally it can reduce stress and anxiety.

Sage can help us feel less anxious and more grounded when life is too hectic or overwhelming. It can also enhance one's inner wisdom.

Violet the sweet flower is a great ally to help alleviate anger or resentment we may be holding onto, particularly if it involves others.

Other:

Compass has been used to show us the way especially when lost.

Phoenix is a symbol of rebirth, resurrection, and renewal. The cycles of life and death, being reborn from its ashes.

Trees represent the changing of seasons and the cycle of life.

Water is a symbol of purification, cleansing, and renewal in many cultures. It's constantly changing form, washing away the old and creating something new.

Chapter 10

Clarity and Confidence

We all can use a little boost in our life whether you have a big project to work on or a very busy time. Maybe you have a huge presentation you have to do. While you can just need clarity, confidence, or willpower for this time you can also have these all work together.

The best part about manifesting these is that it does not counteract anything. You are not trying to force anyone to do anything. It builds you up to hopefully get the outcome you want. Having clarity does not stop you from having more confidence nor the will to make hard decisions.

Being able to walk with confidence in who you are and what you do is a powerful thing. Or maybe you just need enough confidence to do a presentation or have that difficult conversation. Sometimes we just want to be a little better then we are to help us with our lives. To not get stepped all over.

Though I feel like clarity is not exactly the same as focus or attention as it can be made with mostly the same ingredients and a lot of the same intentions. It is having a fog being lifted away and truly seeing. Whether it is an undeniable truth or just everything around you for what it is.

I don't know if you've had a moment when you had someone betray you. Finally catching them talking about you behind your back and the moment on clarity. Seeing them for who they are when you felt something was off. Wondering why other people were treating you a little differently or being told one thing from one person but something else from another. That moment of betrayal but absolute trust opens your eyes to everything around you.

Though I hope you don't have to go through that. There are good moments like that also. Like when you are trying to find the right moves to a dance piece. It just feels off so you just keep throwing moves in there. Then something just clicks. The music feels right and you feel whole in your body.

When you have those moments of clarity or confidence you never want to let them go. Going back is not an option. It is a betrayal to yourself. So you fight to keep it.

Confidence Boost Jar

We could all use a confidence boost. To talk to the cool person and try to make a new friend, or post the photo you like but are self-conscious of putting it out there. Clear quartz is always a good start then carnelian, hematite, and tiger's eye. Rosemary and sage are easy to come by, and I like to add honeysuckle when available.

Other things you can put with this jar are people who you admire. Not for their body type or make you feel guilty for what you don't have. Who inspire you.

Some good places to place this jar is where you get ready in the morning or where you are more critical of yourself. If its at the bathroom mirror or near your closet. Maybe its where you sit with your computer or phone to scroll social media.

I am capable of doing hard things.
I grow with every challenge

Crystal:

Carnelian boosts confidence and courage and is

strongly believed to restore motivation and promote self-esteem.

Clear Quartz enhances focus by clearing mental fog, improving concentration, and promoting a sense of clarity.

Hematite can help to strengthen your self-confidence and balance your aura. It helps to eliminate stress and excess worry or fear.

Lapis Lazuli can help you remember your true power. Helping those who seek clarity of thinking.

Orange calcite can boost mental clarity, creative expression, harmony, and positivity.

Rhodonite brings acceptance by releasing emotional blockages. By accepting yourself your confidence will go up.

Ruby is a stone for action and for momentum. It will help you stay focused and dedicated towards all that you want to manifest in your life.

Sodalite can give you mental clarity for self-expression and to speak your truth.

Tiger's Eye encourages you to be seen in situations where you would otherwise want to hide or blend in. It helps you step into your power and manifest.

Turquoise aids in truth-seeking and manifestation. Assisting people in voicing their opinions and communicating better with people around them.

Herbs:

Cloves can give courage and strength.

Cedar supports us on spiritual quests by reconnecting and grounding us with earthly roots. On a spiritual level has helped them build confidence and courage.

Honeysuckle promotes joy, wonder, and enthusiasm while raising self-esteem and confidence.

Fennel Seeds are often used to promote mental clarity and reduce mental clutter, contributing to a state of relaxed alertness.

Nutmeg can improve overall clarity and 'peace of mind'.

Orange Lilies are representations of confidence.

Peppermint is great for sharpening your memory, focus, and cognitive function.

Rosemary is often used for manifestation and protection. It can also enhance cognitive function, sharpen your memory, and boost your overall confidence.

Sage is often used in manifestation rituals to clear negative energy and promote a positive mindset.

Tarragon can increase self-confidence.

Yarrow protects from enchanting distractions. It can also help to provide clarity and discernment.

Other:

Lion is a symbol of strength and confidence.

Peacock is a bright and flamboyant bird. They are associated with royalty, grace, and confidence.

Red Candle uses color magic representing strength and confidence.

Chapter 11

Intuition and Magical Abilities

We all have a little bit of magic in us. Its up to us to figure out how it manifests into the world. Now, this is not the book to figure this out. In the resources in the end I'll have some books you can check out to get started. But we all have our own intuition and we need to listen to it because it just wants to protect us.

We all have intuition and can do things to strengthen it. Having a jar or satchel of items specific for it can't hurt.

There are plenty of other abilities that you can make spell jars for; prophetic dreams, clairvoyance, astral projection just to name a few. Of course these are for strengthening gifts that you already have. Sadly we cannot poof ourselves into pyromancy.

For some they may need to use tools to use their

gifts. This can be reading with tarot or oracle cards, a pendulum, tea leaves, dreams, and many others. Even if you use a crystal ball its nice to have something to give yourself a little extra oomph. Now with these I do not mix these with protection ingredients. Even though some of them overlap. Make sure to have one that is separate.

You do not want all these other energies mixing together for something so important as yours and others' protection. So I always have one separate container that is specific just for that alone. It is dedicated to that alone with salt and a candle. Participially so I can see if something happens to it. Like a crack or the candle burns weird. That means it did its job, something tried to get through and you need to get rid of all of the biodegradable thing (most likely not the crystals) and remake the jar.

If you are part of a particular belief system you may have some rituals or spells you do also. These should not interfere with those since they are made beforehand and are more a passive presence. Just make sure it is out of the way.

There will be other books you can look up to really dive into about this. Whether if you want to know more, train into it, or just have a better understanding to make your spells. Then you can determine what ingredients to use from there.

Dream Jar

This can be if you want to have lucid dreams, prophetic dreams or just prevent nightmares. A good base is amethyst, clear quartz, and selenite. Some of my favorites also are moonstone, rainbow flourite, bay leaves, calendula, and carnations. The nice thing about all of these is if you do not get anything prophetic you at least get restful sleep.

Other things you can do to help is to have a good night routine. Having such chaos just before you go to bed is not good for sleep with not good for receiving any *gifts*. Wash your face and wind down. Don't have you face stuck from one screen to the next to the next until you pass out. This is not even an age thing. My dad will be on his laptop for hour then scroll his phone and have the TV on until he passes out at night. And he wonders why he's still tired in the morning and his neck hurts.

Taking care of yourself allows for your gifts to come through. You won't remember what your dreams are if you are too exhausted in the morning. You can barely remember where you put your keys.

I am in control of my dreams, and I manifest my desires effortlessly

My lucid dreams are a playground for manifesting my goals

Crystals:

Amazonite is for emotional intelligence and intuition.

Amethyst is great for developing your intuition. It aligns with the heart chakra, which is the highest level of spiritual awareness and actualization. Opens the third eye, allowing space to raise your consciousness.

Apatite helps to lead to a higher consciousness and increase energy. It can help regulate energy flow and prevent burnout.

Beryl opens the crown and solar plexus chakra, stimulating adaptability, activity and vitality. It is known as the Seer Stone because it is excellent for developing scrying skills.

Clear quartz opens your psychic communications but still adds protection. Heightens your intuition and sensitivity to spirit.

Fluorite encourages clarity and helps you to connect with yourself.

Kyanite is said to be helpful for those who wish to develop their psychic abilities, such as clairvoyance, clairsentience, and clairaudience. It is also used for strengthening your intuition and tarot reading.

Labradorite stimulate the Third Eye chakra,

enhancing psychic abilities, clairvoyance, and telepathic communication.

Lapis lazuli helps with opening your third eye.

Malachite can be use for psychic protection and development.

Moonstone can activate your intuition which is connected to psychic abilities. It is also a powerful aid to manifesting your magic and channeling This stone is known to aid in focus, awareness, and even to enhance psychic powers.

Selenite crystals are associated with the moon and are known for their ability to promote intuition and psychic abilities. They are also thought to be helpful in promoting peace, calmness, and relaxation. Great for cleansing.

Sodalite is a great crystal for clairvoyance and connecting with your spirit guides

Herbs:

Angelica can aid in visions and protection. It also creates harmony and courage and have been use in exorcisms.

Bay Leaf increases psychic powers. Also brings in protection, healing, success, purification, strength, and wisdom.

Calendula (which is also called marigold) increases psychic and spiritual powers, and aid prophetic dreams. It can dispel negativity too.

Carnation can provide enhancement for magical

powers, protection, strength, healing, and achieving balance.

Damiana enhances intuition and psychic abilities. It is a natural relaxant, helping to alleviate anxiety and stress. When a person is less anxious and more relaxed, we have seen that they may be more open to intuitive or psychic insights.

Mugwort has a long history of use in various cultures for an ability to stimulate vivid dreams and enhance lucid dreaming it also enhance one's connection to the spiritual world and facilitate psychic experiences.

Yarrow amplifies psychic powers and enhances divination. It also strengthens the aura and a strong auric field provides protection and enhances one's ability to perceive and interact with spiritual or psychic realms.

Other:

Water can be used not in the jar but around it as a reflection to charge to add energy when you are first building and when recharging.

Bells have been use in many belief systems as protections and cleansing.

Mirror used for spells and glamour for centuries. Many beliefs would even have them covered when not in use because they could be used as portals.

Moon or any representation of the moon. Even in

ancient times the moon seen as a representation of dreams and magic.

Pentagram or other symbols of you belief systems can be good here too that represents trusting yourself, intuition, or magic.

Chapter 12

Happiness, Peace, Luck

Now, some of these may seem like things are overlapping, and they kind of are. Sometimes magic is not an exact science. Parts of it is for safety reason and others you just go with a feeling. But with how the world is going right now we all could use a little more happiness and peace, even just in our own little worlds.

Adding a little luck into your life may just be breaking a bad streak or turning things around in your life. That no matter what you do in your life something seems to go wrong. Even with every great thing that happens something small will put a damper on it. Or every time you get farther in life something always seems to pull you back just a little bit.

Not to say that we don't sabotage ourselves. We

can't just expect magic to fix all our problems. We can get the energy out there to help us along but we still need to do the work. This is just the added a boost to cut out the outside influence messing with us.

This is different then the next chapter of grief and loss. Its almost like someone is trying to sabotage things for you, a frenemy. You want to just have a little something more for yourself in life. Nothing is horrible, but things could be better.

As with most things, like attracts like. Being a debbie downer won't really help to bring luck into your life. Or always wanting bad things to happen to others won't really bring peace to you. Can't expect love and happiness in one part of your life then lob a grenade in another part.

You need to work on yourself at the same time.

Taking some 'me' time is great for sitting at home watching your favorite shows or reading your favorite book (or thing online). But the flip side is that sometime you do need to go outside. Put on some sunscreen and get some natural vitamin D. Gasp, talk to people.

Maybe it just you need to journal some things on a regular basis to see the patterns in your life. Have time to feel grateful for what you have. Talk to that good friend you always has a good thing to say and not the co-worker who always complains. Maybe even work through some shadow work (reference).

The luck and happiness you have is also what you bring in and what you allow into your life. If others always have things bad maybe they are bring it in to you too. Not saying you should drop every single person like that in your life, but maybe on top of working on yourself you protect yourself. Not just magically.

This is getting into the therapy side of things. Not my specialty.

Good Luck Jar

Having good luck coming into your home and to everyone into your home is always a good thing. Some good crystals to start with are carnelian, green aventurine, and jade. I find that chamomile and lavender work very well together magically. Plus the scents do not clash.

Citrine and peach moonstone are good additions. Also they are pretty additions and make me happy. You can never go wrong with a four leave clover. I know some people who have some charms in theirs that were given to them. Even better if was someone you believe is "luckier" or farther in life then you are.

I am grateful for the blessings and abundance that surround me, and I attract even more happiness and joy into my life.

I am worthy of happiness and joy, and I allow myself to experience the full spectrum of positive emotions.

I am a lucky person, and luck follows me wherever I go.

Crystals:

Aquamarine allows you to tap into the depths of your emotions and experience tranquility and calm. It can also counter feelings of being overwhelmed. It is a calming stone that can bolster courage and strength.

Carnelian is the magnet for good luck and prosperity. It can also provide protection that helps deflect negative energy while also providing emotional support.

Citrine can help you to release feelings of stress and overwhelm, and promote feelings of joy and happiness. It has the pow of positivity abundance, and luck.

Flower Agate is all about growth, joy, and inner peace. It has the magic of pure magic, hope, and happiness.

Green Aventurine can bring in good luck and health, prosperity, success, and opportunity.

Jade is one of Chinese culture's most vital good luck crystals. Its ability to attract luxury and happiness has been renowned worldwide for ages.

Orange Calcite is a crystal that embodies sunshine. It's all about uplifting energy, confidence, and creativity. Everything you need to feel happy and fulfilled.

Peach Moonstone has a gentle energy can help to promote positive feelings from within, while also enhancing your sense of self-worth and confidence. It can help you let go of stress and anxiety, allowing you to focus on the present moment and find inner peace

Pyrite brings happiness, success, prosperity, and abundance. It has a warm and welcoming energy that can help to promote feelings of joy and positivity from within, while also enhancing your sense of self-worth and confidence.

Sunstone can awaken your inner strength, radiate positivity, and attract happiness into your life.

Tiger's Eye is associated with happiness, strength, and courage. It is said to have a grounding energy that can help to promote feelings of stability and security, while also enhancing our self-confidence and courage.

Herbs

Basil is believed to bring luck, prosperity, and protection.

Bay Leaves as a symbol of triumph and peace to ancient Romans

Catnip draws love, luck and happiness,

Chamomile can bring good luck and fortune if you use the whole flower.

Lavender is not only great smelling but also brings luck, peace, and happiness

Marjoram was known to the Romans as the herb of happiness, and was believed to increase lifespan.

Vervain can bring peace, love, and happiness

Other:

Peace Sign is pretty self explanatory. Any other symbols that represent this to you can work as well.

Four Leaf Clover are a symbol for luck. Not only the herb but the representation of it can be used.

Chapter 13

Grief and Feeling Lost

This chapter is a little different then wanting just peace. Grief is its own beast in itself. It tears a chunk out of you that you will not get back and you have to learn how to live without it. These kinds of baby steps can feel like you walking through mud while having no air in your lungs. There is no doing one small thing each day because sometimes just existing is enough.

Feeling lost is also something else entirely. It is hard to explain unless you have gone through it yourself. It is a sense of having no sense of self. Not feeling like you are all together here. You know that you are physically in this world but not solid. So you try to find things to fill the holes. Which can easily turn bad because you are just taking whatever is around you that is "not you".

Both have you searching for something. You do the best you can not to drown and not take others down with you. To heal in a healthy way while you take the needed time to go through this. Do not feel like you need to go faster because it makes others uncomfortable or that you need to be "normal" because society thinks enough time has passed. Pushing through can also hurt you.

Believe me, it is hard to go through. It is lonely. And you will have to go it alone. Even if others are feeling the same loss you are all going through your own journey and it will not be the same. You can help each other when and where you can but you need to know that sometimes it will not be enough. On either end.

You will get push back. Others will want you to be "normal" just so they don't have to feel uncomfortable anymore. Now there will be times you will have to fake it. You have responsibilities you can't ignore like children and bills. But around those, no.

You get to be selfish.

Take your time. Heal.

Grief Jar

I have made this a jar as well as a pouch. Mostly because it with be touched, a lot. Not always by you, but if you do not wants others to touch it then make sure it is somewhere that others cannot see and maybe do not tell them what it is for. It is simple and not made of fragile things.

I actually made one recently at the passing of my beloved Enzo in the winter of 2024. It wasn't a complete surprise, he was at the upper age of his dog breed but he did go kind of quickly. But losing a pet is never easy so I hope this will help you in some way.

I had this jar sitting next to a photo of him, his collar, and later his ashes. It was a comfort to have something that could be moved and touched that didn't feel so precious that I would somehow damage by handling too much. These were there for me and were meant for my comfort.

I personally did not put in lava stone because I took the stones out to feel. Did have amethyst, black obsidian, and Botswana agate. The same with thyme, it crumbled too much. Rosemary and rose petals held up much better. The same thing if you decide on using a pouch to carry around. Other things to place inside are pieces that the person (place/thing/or whatever it bothering you) found important within.

I placed a rock from his favorite park in the jar. For a friend I found a charm of her sister's favorite book and got her two. One for the jar and one she could interchange onto any of her jewelry. Another person could gather water from a beloved beach and seal it into a tiny container.

The best part about these jars is that once your grief has dissipated enough you do not have to throw it away. It can just sit as decoration. The spell has done its work, but not all has to completely dismantled to be "properly" done.

My grief is normal and right
My feelings matter
I breathe in peace and acceptance
Joy and grief can coexist

Crystals:

Apache Tears do not make the grief go away but will help you process it in a healthy way. Bringing comfort, calm, and emotional healing.

Amber instills a sense of comfort, also associated with health and protection.

Amethyst can help restore inner peace and emotional stability. It can help release painful emotions and it promotes a sense of calm and serenity.

Black Obsidian is also known as the "grief stone" as it is thought to be very helpful for those dealing with loss or healing trauma. If held during meditation it can help unblock buried feelings of grief allowing the healing process to start.

Green Apatite works with the heart chakra which can help you deal with grief or sadness over the loss of a loved one. Encouraging growth and improvement in your health and well-being.

Botswana Agate is soothing to those who are lonely, easily hurt or grieve a loss. Great for those who need comfort and strength in trying times.

Hiddenite is great as an overall comfort for emotional problems, including grief, loss, and heartbreak.

Howlite lets you touch the harder emotions found in our loss. It digs deep so you cannot hide from it and actually face so that you can face the grief.

Lava Stone is a grounding stone that is believed to provide physical and emotional strength when facing difficult situations.

Lepidolite can help you get stable footing. Finding balance when you are blind in your emotions.

Rhodonite is a very supportive stone that helps with rediscovering one's inner gifts. Stimulating acceptance and forgiveness toward self and others.

Ruby can help you heal your heart when it is deeply wounded.

Snowflake obsidian is good for grounding, releasing negative emotions, and easing anxiety.

Tree Agate is a grounding and protective crystal giving a calming peace that helps those during a period of bereavement.

Herbs:

Calendula is a happiness herb and can bring

optimism and vitality to your life. It can cleanse negative energies. It can also aid in with grief and sadness.

Lavender is one of the best for helping with promoting happiness and healing depression. The scent alone can be uplifting.

Rose has long been used to comfort and soothe the heart. It also has a gentle antidepressant and sedative properties which can your emotions while proving a sense of ease.

Rosemary is tied to memory, remembrance, and things of the past. It reminds us to hold in our hearts those things that are no longer with us but to live in the present and look towards the future.

Sage is a plant with enormous spiritual power. It is great to grounding, clearing, and cleansing. It builds emotional strength and may help to heal grief.

Thyme helps us hold space for our grief. It reminds us to make time (no pun intended) for it, work through our feels, and ultimately come to accept it.

Other:

Parts of your loved one is pretty self explanatory. It can be their ashes or something that represents them. Even something that they loved.

Pictures of the thing you cared about or a moment to represent that person or time that gives you comfort.

Chapter 14

Health

All we have is ourselves and we need our health. So to live a long life we need to stay healthy to enjoy it. This chapter will be a bit jumbled since there are so many areas related to your health. I will cover as much as I can, but will mostly keep to general stuff.

Of course if you have a real medical problem please go to a professional. These should be be used in conjunction and anything that will be ingestion should be consulted with your doctor first. Honestly, nothing here should be ingested. I don't know you people and how well you won't cross-contaminate things. There are many things that can counteract with medication, even everyday foods and herbs.

Please don't die.

Your health is one of the most important things. You cannot live life to the fullest if you do not feel well. That much I know very well with a recent chronic illness that finally got figured out. So much of your life is hindered. You cannot work or go out to see friends and family. So you can't make money or socialize. So you are stressed about bills and socializing is down to zero. And relaxing at home to recharge can't really happen because of all the stress plus the health problems.

It just turns into a vicious cycle. The usual things to make yourself feel better don't work because it's not a "normal" thing wrong. There is a lot in the world that's fighting against us right now.

I'm not going to get all social justice, 'corporations-are-poisoning-us' but just know that there is a lot out there. We don't know what's going on. There is only so much you can do as an individual with eating healthy and taking care of yourself. After a while you look outside yourself for help, for some its spiritual (again please seek medical professional help).

Check out the chapter on Resources for books on Herbalism for more info about herbs and plants to add into your practice and when and if you use them medicinally. Those books will also have further readings to give you as well.

Healthy Home

A good base for this jar is hemetite and rose quartz. Adding in clear quartz to any spell will enhance it, amethyst because why not, and emerald seems to be hitting a lot of areas. I personally like to have ginger and echinacea mostly because I always have some around. Work smarter, not harder.

You can have this in your bedroom to work on you when you sleep. In the kitchen since that is where you get your food that nourishes you. Or whatever room you spent the most time in. Which could be the living room or an office or even the kitchen.

Good health is my divine right.
My body is capable of healing.
My body is a temple of health and vitality.
I am worthy of good health and well-being.

Crystals:

Amazonite is known for maintaining good health in general. It aids in cell regeneration and healing after illnesses, injury, and trauma.

Amethyst can ease all kinds of aches and pains especially headaches and migraines. It can help facilitate good healthy sleep and grants positive power to those trying to move away from addictions.

Aventurine for helping to speed up recovery and keeping your system healthy. It supports your whole system (with an emphasis on the heart and the blood).

Black Tourmaline will boost immunity and circulation, to cutting down on aches and pains and even improving the respiratory system. It also shields against EMF's.

Carnelian gives your energy levels a kick and get you motivated, whether its your body or your mind. It can also be helpful to your blood circulation and fertility issues.

Citrine can bring a burst of energy and detox the body. Also helping to treat depression and anxiety.

Emerald is believed to address heart, lung, and muscular ailments, expediting the healing process and promoting recovery.

Garnet is associated with fortifying your immune system, boosting energy levels, and enhancing overall well-being.

Hemetite promotes circulation, eases anxiety, and enhances mental clarity. It's great for blood conditions especially anemia. Supports the kidneys and regenerates tissue, but overall physical and mental well-being.

Lapis Lazuli encourages good sleep so the body can heal.

Moonstone eases PMS and supporting fertility or hormonal change journeys.

Pyrite helps to keep us safe from pollutants, EMF's, and anything that would cause us damage.

Rose Quartz keeps your heart and circulation in check physically; emotionally it makes sure that you are living in harmony and making loving decisions that will serve you well.

Herbs:

Arugula can help with fertility and your overall health.

Chamomile is uses for purification and protection. Used for anxiety and sleep.

Echinacea (coneflower) can boost immune function, relieve pain, reduce inflammation, and have hormonal, antiviral, and antioxidant effects.

Elder give protection and could take away fever. It is also ground to help you through trauma and grief.

Ginger is good for overall health and well-being. I know I said earlier not to ingest anything but this is a great food to add in and protection from evil.

Lavender is a natural healer and the scent alone can help with aches and pains. Easing stress and anxiety.

Marjoram is calming a soothing.

Rosemary is good for sleep and purification. It can also help with improving your memory.

Other:

Salt has been used for protection and purifying. It is also a good solid base for any spell.

Animals have been seen as symbols in many cultures for good health. The wolf and bear for American

Indigenous tribes, bats for China, and lion and giraffe for Africa just to name a few.

Chapter 15

Not Truely An End

I hope you had fun going through this book and creating these jars. Making them your own. Experimenting to see what works for you and just mixing with other things that works in your practice.

This is just the beginning. Continue to work on your spell work. Study more on what excites you in your practice and see what can be incorporated. There is so much more to learn out there. Some of it will be from others but a lot of it will be practice yourself. Trial and error (safely) will be your friend.

Keep this book as a reference or pass it on to another later on when you feel like you don't need it anymore.

Doing The Work

You do not need to feel like you need to study and do spell work every day. This is not school. There is no homework. We are all adults (even if you are not I'm giving you permission to have this freedom) and can decide what we do with our time. We have lives. Other responsibilities and things we love. Plus there are only so many hours in the day. Don't over burden yourself.

Even though it is called spell 'work' it doesn't mean you have to clock in so many hours. The gods are not tallying things against you. no matter what you have been taught before, there is no 'sin' in anything you do. Your practice should be a part of your play time. Just like how you would read or watch a movie at home. This is something you can do for fun.

It is up to you how much of your practice is spiritual or not. I kept it very nonsecular of really any kind of belief base so you could fit it in more easily into your life. All of this can be used for any belief or no belief system. Even if you are still exploring it will still come with you.

Magic just is.

It is not given to you by some god or from some elaborate ritual. some belief systems out there do have initiations, but that is to get in for them. not for magic. that is yous and yous alone. It exists everywhere and touches everything. It cannot be taken from you. You just need to go outside to feel it if you are feeling lost.

Chapter 16

Resources

Spells and Crafting

Black, Lyra. *Recreational Witchcraft: No-nonsense Witchcraft for the Everyday Modern Witch* (Liminal 11, 2022)

Dugan, Ellen. Book of Witchery: *Spells, Charms & Correspondences for Every Day of the Week* (Llewellyn Publications, 2009)

Gonzalez-Wippler, Migene. *The Complete Book of Amulets and Talismans* (Llewellyn Publications, 1991)

Lovelace, Amanda. *Make Your Own Magic: A Beginner's Guide To Self-Empowering Witchcraft* (New York: Hachette Book Group 2024)

Crystals

Eason, Cassandra. *1001 Crystal: The Complete Book*

of *Crystals for Every Purpose* (New York; Sterling Publishing Co 2023)

Dunwich, Gerina. *Gemstone and Crystal Magic: A Modern Witch's Guide to Using Stones for Spells, Amulets, Rituals, and Divination* (Weiser Books, 2022)

Hall, Judy. *The Crystal Bible* (Krause Publications, 2003)

Lembo, Margaret Ann. *The Essential Guide to Crystals, Minerals and Stones* (Llewellyn Publications, 2013)

Herbalism

Cunningham, Scott. *Cunningham's Encyclopedia of Magical Herbs* (Llewellyn Publications, 1985)

Dugan, Ellen. *Garden Witchery: Magick from the Ground Up (Ellen Dugan's Garden Witchery, 1)* (Llewellyn Publications, 2003)

Morrison, Dorothy. *Bud, Blossom & Leaf: The Magical Herb Gardener's Handbook* (Llewellyn Publications, 2001)

Nock, Judy Ann. *The Modern Witchcraft Guide to Magickal Herbs: Your Complete Guide to the Hidden Powers of Herbs (Modern Witchcraft Magic, Spells, Rituals)* (Adams Media, 2019)

Sigils and Signs

Zakroff, Laura Tempest. *Sigil Witchery: A Witch's*

Guide to Crafting Magick Symbols (Llewellyn Publications, 2018)

Nock, Judy Ann. *The Modern Witchcraft Guide to Runes: Your Complete Guide to the Divination Power of Runes (Modern Witchcraft Magic, Spells, Rituals)* (Adams Media, 2022)

Gods and Goddesses

Blair, Nancy. The Goddess Book: *A Celebration of Witches, Queens, Healers, and Crones* (Hampton Roads Publishing, 2021)

Conway, D.J. *Magick of the Gods and Goddesses: How to Invoke their Powers* (Llewellyn Publications, 2020)

Anung is a fiction and non-fiction author, and poet. You can find more of that at anungvilay.com.

She also runs her irreverent shop of pins, stickers, and apparel at Inspite Shop.

Eclectic green witch who's always been solo, but will join in at random conferences.

She is also the host of The Introvert's Bubble and I Don't Wanna Fit In podcasts. Serial starter and dreamer.

She lives in Minnesota. Dog lover. Constantly reading, writing, and creating.

Watercolor illustrations by Maria Barbieri
(Spell jars, including cover)   www.mariabpaints.com

www.ingramcontent.com/pod-product-compliance
Lightning Source LLC
LaVergne TN
LVHW012243070526
838201LV00090B/108